TIGERS

Written and edited by **Barbara Taylor Cork**

Consultant Miranda Stevenson BA PhD
Curator of Animals, Royal Zoological Society of Scotland

Two-Can Publishing Ltd

First published in Great Britain in 1989 by
Two-Can Publishing Ltd
27 Cowper Street
London EC2A 4AP

© Two-Can Publishing Ltd., 1989

Text by Barbara Taylor Cork
Design by David Bennett

Printed and bound by Purnells, England

All rights reserved. No part of this publication may be reproduced, stored in a retrieval system, or transmitted in any form or by any means, electronic, mechanical, photocopying, recording or otherwise, without prior written permission of the copyright owner.

British Library Cataloguing in Publication Data

Tigers.
 1. Tigers — For children
 599.74'428

ISBN 1-85434-080-3

Photograph Credits:
p.4 (top) Bruce Coleman/Gerald Cubitt (bottom) Bruce Coleman/Ron Boardman Jacana/Fréderique p.5 Ardea/Charles McDougal p.6 (top) Zefa/K. H. Kurz p.6 (bottom) Bruce Coleman/Peter Jackson p.7 Ardea/Charles McDougal p.8/9 G. Ziesler p.9 (inset) G. Ziesler p.10/11 Zefa/Horus p.12 Bruce Coleman/G. Ziesler p.13 Frank Spooner Pictures p.14 Ardea/Richard Waller p.15 (top) Bruce Coleman/Dieter and Mary Plage (bottom) Zefa p.16 (top) Ardea/Ian Beames p.16 (bottom) Ardea/Charles McDougal p.17 (top) Ardea/Charles McDougal p.17 (bottom) Ardea/Charles McDougal Cover photo Z. Leszcynski

Illustration Credits:
p.1 Malcolm Livingstone p.3 Malcolm Livingstone/Alan Rogers p.7 Malcolm Livingstone p.8 Malcolm Livingstone p.10-11 Malcolm Livingstone p.13 Malcolm Livingstone p.18-19 Alastair Graham p.20-24 David Cook p.25 Alan Rogers p.27 Claire Legemah p.28-29 Malcolm Livingstone p.30 Tony Wells p.31 Alan Rogers p.32 Malcolm Livingstone

CONTENTS

Looking at tigers	4
Where do tigers live?	6
Hunting for food	8
A tiger's day	10
Finding a mate	12
Baby tigers	13
Family life	14
Growing up	16
Save the tiger	17
Jungle game	18
A first for tiger	20
Spot the difference	25
Tiger mask	26
Find the tigers	28
Tiger stripe maze	30
True or false?	31
Index	32

LOOKING AT TIGERS

A tiger is a fierce, strong cat that hunts in forests and jungles. Tigers are the biggest cats in the world. A male tiger may be longer than a car and weigh more than two adult men. A tiger's tail is nearly 0.6 metres (2 feet) long.

Female tigers are smaller than the males. A female tiger is called a tigress. Apart from their size, male and female tigers look the same. They both have orange fur with thick, black stripes.

Tigers are the only big cats that are striped all over. What sort of patterns do other big cats, such as leopards or jaguars, have on their fur?

▶ When a tiger walks, it pulls up its claws inside its toes. This stops the claws wearing down and getting blunt.

▲ Some tigers are born without any orange in their fur. These white tigers are very rare but some of them are kept in zoos.

TIGER FACES

Every tiger has a different pattern of black stripes on its face. Can you see the differences between the patterns on these two faces? The face markings help scientists to tell one tiger from another.

WHERE DO TIGERS LIVE?

Tigers can live in cold, snowy mountains and forests as well as hot jungles, grasslands and swamps. Nowadays, most tigers live in India and other parts of Southeast Asia. Tigers are not very common anywhere in the world.

The beautiful black stripes on a tiger's coat match the patterns on the trees, bushes and grasses. This helps it to creep close to the animals it hunts without being seen.

▼ In long grass, if a tiger keeps quite still, it is very hard to see.

▲ Siberian tigers live in very cold, snowy places. They have long, shaggy fur, which helps them to keep warm.

Tigers live on their own for most of the time. A tiger does not make a home but each one lives in its own special area. This is called its territory and it has to be large enough to give the tiger food, water and shelter.

A tiger marks its territory with scent, droppings and scrape marks. It also roars from time to time. A tiger's roars can be heard up to 3.2 kilometres (2 miles) away. These smells, marks and sounds usually tell other tigers, "I live here, keep out".

◀ A tiger's paw prints are called pug marks. They show how big the tiger is and how fast it was moving.

TRACKING A TIGER

▼ Scars on trees show where a tiger cleans and sharpens its claws. Have you seen a pet cat do this? A tiger's claws are so sharp they cut through the bark like knives.

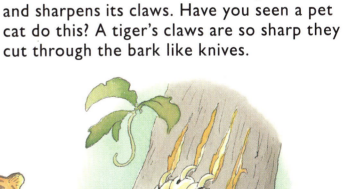

▲ A tiger sprays scent at certain places along the paths in its territory. The scent is a mixture of urine and a smelly liquid, which comes from two glands under the tail.

HUNTING FOR FOOD

Tigers usually hunt at night. They spend a lot of time searching for food. A tiger's favourite food is deer and wild pigs but it will eat any animals it can catch, from monkeys and peacocks to buffalo and goats.

A tiger has many weapons to help it to catch its food. It has long, pointed front teeth, sharp, curved claws and powerful shoulders.

But a tiger has to work hard for its meals. It can't run as fast as many of the animals it hunts so it has to get quite close to them before it pounces.

▶ This tiger is getting ready to pounce on a deer. If the deer escapes, the tiger will go hungry. Often, a tiger will not catch anything to eat for a week.

FOOD FACTS

Tigers seem to enjoy eating rotting meat, even when it's full of maggots.

One tiger can move a whole cow on its own.

CATCHING A DEER

● When a tiger sees a deer, it freezes quite still. Then it crouches close to the ground.

● The tiger creeps forward very slowly and quietly until it is close to the deer.

● Suddenly, the tiger pounces. It knocks the deer over and sinks its teeth into the deer's neck.

● The tiger drags the deer to a shady place and starts to feed. Its sharp cheek teeth help to cut up the meat.

▲ A tiger takes several days to eat a big animal.

A TIGER'S DAY

During the day, a tiger spends most of the time resting or sleeping in the shade.

When a tiger is thirsty, it laps up water just like a pet cat laps up a saucer of milk.

In hot weather, a tiger loves to sit in water or have a swim. A tiger is a very good swimmer.

A tiger smooths its fur back into place with its tongue. This is called grooming.

FINDING A MATE

A male tiger and a tigress come together for mating. When a tigress is looking for a mate, she roars loudly. Male tigers living nearby roar back and go to find the tigress. They find her by her roars and the scent marks she leaves along the paths.

Male tigers may fight fierce battles over a tigress. They charge at each other and fight with their sharp teeth and claws. The strongest tiger wins the fight and will mate with the tigress.

When two tigers meet each other, they often make a soft, puffing noise. They also touch cheeks or rub the sides of their bodies against each other. A pet cat behaves in the same way when it rubs against a person's legs to say "Hello" and show it is friendly.

BABY TIGERS

About 14 weeks after mating, a tigress may have some babies. The babies are called cubs and 3-4 cubs are usually born at one time. They are blind, helpless and very small; they weigh only about 1.5 kilograms (3 pounds).

The tigress hides the newborn cubs in a safe place, such as in a cave, under a fallen tree or in a patch of very thick grass. The cubs may be killed if enemies such as jackals or hyenas find them.

▶ At first, the cubs spend most of the time asleep or sucking milk from their mother. After one or two weeks, their eyes open but they can only see things close to them.

CUB FACTS

When a tiger cub is born, it weighs less than half as much as a human baby.

If the cubs are in danger, the tigress will move them to a safe place. She carries each cub in her mouth.

A tigress may give birth to up to 7 cubs at a time.

Tiger cubs drink their mother's milk until they are about 6 months old.

FAMILY LIFE

The cubs grow fast. By the time the cubs are 6 weeks old, they weigh 4.5 kg (10 pounds). They have their first meals of meat, which their mother catches for them. They soon start to follow their mother on hunting trips. They sleep in different places and don't have a home to go back to each day.

When the cubs are out with their mother, they have to do as she tells them and keep well hidden while she hunts for food. They may have to wait for days until she comes back to lead them to a meal.

When a mother tigress wants her cubs to follow her, she makes some soft grunting noises which mean "Follow me". If a cub loses its mother, it calls "miaow" loudly. If her cubs are attacked, a tigress will defend them fiercely.

The family usually feeds at night. The tigress makes sure that there is no danger before she lets the cubs have their dinner. As well as the meat, the tigers eat most of the skin and the small bones.

The biggest and strongest cub usually gets the best feeding spot. It growls to keep the other cubs away. If there is a lot of meat, each cub gets a share. But if there is not much food, the weakest cubs often go hungry. They may even die of starvation.

▼ A tigress watches over her cubs while they drink.

▲ The cubs have to learn the best way to eat an animal, such as this deer.

GROWING UP

As the cubs grow older, they learn more and more. They copy their mother and play stalking and pouncing games with their brothers and sisters. This helps them to learn how to catch food and take care of themselves.

When the cubs are about a year old, their mother starts to teach them how to hunt. They have to learn when to pounce on an animal and the best way to kill it.

At this stage, the mother tiger begins to leave the cubs on their own for a few days at a time so they will learn more about how to survive on their own. When the cubs are about two years old, they leave their family to look for their own special area of forest or jungle. Perhaps, one day, they will be mothers or fathers themselves.

▲ A tiger walks on tiptoe and can glide through the jungle without making a sound.

SAVE THE TIGER

Today, there are only about 5000 tigers left in the wild. Years ago, there were a lot more tigers than this but people killed many of the tigers and cut down the forests where they lived. The people needed the land to build villages and grow food.

In the 1970s, the World Wide Fund for Nature started 'Project Tiger' to help tigers to survive. Areas of land in India were made into nature reserves to give the tigers room to live in peace. People are not allowed to kill tigers in a nature reserve. Many countries stopped buying tiger skins so fewer tigers were made into rugs and coats.

As a result of this work, as well as the breeding of tigers in zoos, the numbers of tigers are now increasing. But more still needs to be done to save the tiger.

▲ This tiger is wearing a radio collar.

▼ These aerials pick up signals from the tiger's radio collar so scientists can track the tiger. The information they collect helps them to plan the best way to help tigers to survive.

A FIRST FOR TIGER

BY CATHERINE RIPLEY

"EEEEEEEKK!" The screech of a distant bird woke Tiger from her late afternoon sleep. She was lying half in and half out of a pool of water. Although she didn't move a muscle, she became suddenly alert. The warning cry from the bird might mean that her mother was returning.

Tiger's mother had been gone for a week. Before she left, she had rubbed her big furry jowls against Tiger's. "Prrruuu..." she had puffed, and then she had rustled through the dry, dead leaves of the bare forest and down the hillside.

Tiger had been waiting patiently

for her return. The two had often gone hunting together so that Tiger could practise her stalking techniques under her mother's watchful eye. But sometimes her mother had left her alone. At first, the young tigress had thought it was just another of these long absences. Before, her mother had always returned to lead her cub to a kill. This time was different. Somehow Tiger sensed her mother was not coming back.

Deep inside, Tiger's stomach rumbled and grumbled. She was starving. For the last few nights she had tried to hunt – leaping at a monkey, swatting at a peacock and even shadowing a herd of deer, but with no luck. Tonight she would go farther afield.

The sun was setting now, and the heat of the day was being blown away by a cool evening breeze. With it, the breeze brought a strange, uncomfortable smell. What was it? Tiger pulled herself out of the pool. It smelled dangerous. All at once, the whole forest seemed to be on the run. A flock of lapwings flew across

the nearby clearing. Monkeys swung nervously though the treetops, and a herd of deer burst past. All the animals ignored Tiger — they were trying to escape!

Tiger took the warning. Whatever was making the air cloudy and hard to breathe couldn't be good. Tiger joined the other animals. Behind them, a line of flames appeared. The fire licked at the dry leaves, and in no time at all, it reached the water at a pool. Food!

Tiger raised herself slowly and padded toward them, keeping in the shadows and out of the moonlit patches. She tried to be as quiet as possible. Crackle! She had made a mistake and her foot came down on a dry leaf. The deer turned at the noise, instantly on their guard. "Pok! Pok!" they barked, stamping their hooves. Now that she had been detected, Tiger knew there was no

hole where Tiger had been sleeping.

Several hours later, Tiger sprawled out on top of a rocky hillock. She tried to catch her breath as she looked out over her new surroundings. What she saw pleased her. The forest in the valley showed signs of life. Young trees and bushes were in leaf. This was a welcome change from the bare branches of the hillside where Tiger had come from. Beyond the forest's edge, she could see a group of deer drinking point in pretending she wasn't there. She strode out into the open. The deer trotted away from her and into the forest.

When Tiger reached the water, she took a long deep drink. Then she continued across the meadow to the forest's edge. Here she stopped, lifted her tail and squirted thick milky spray over the trunk of a tree. If this was to be Tiger's new home, it was time to mark out her territory. After marking her path several more

times, she came across a well worn trail. Tiger sniffed and rolled back her lips and nose at the strong smell. A male tiger had been using the trail. He had been here a week or so ago. Would he accept her in his territory?

Suddenly, out of the night there he was walking towards her. They approached each other warily. "Prrruuu..." the big male chuffed, blowing out a deep throaty purr through his half-open lips. "Prrruuu..." Tiger responded. The two cats rubbed against each other and then parted company. The male had accepted Tiger. She could stay, and perhaps in a year or so, they would mate.

Tiger followed a dried-up stream bed that wound its way out of the forest and back into the meadow. It led to a small waterhole under a tall shady tree. Tiger sniffed and looked around her. She sensed that some deer visited this spot regularly. She would wait for them.

Tiger crouched in the middle of a tall clump of grass and stayed motionless. She listened for the

approach of hooves. From time to time she rose to see if there was any movement. It was now three in the morning. In another two hours the

sun would be rising and Tiger would have to go back to the shade of the forest. Tiger was tired and hungry. Would the deer come to drink this morning? And if they did, could she successfully kill one?

One hour passed and then another. The copper red sun began to rise in the eastern sky. Tiger remained hidden and hopeful. Then ever so faintly she heard the hoofbeats of some deer. Perhaps the long wait would pay off after all. Tiger raised her head bit by bit. Across the plain were five spotted deer. Tiger lowered herself down into the grass again. The deer came closer and closer. They stopped and started several times, sensing danger but not able to see it. When the deer were within fifty yards of the pool, they stopped once again. It was now or never!

Tiger leaped out of the grass and with a quick bound, she was upon the deer. Instantly the herd scattered and bolted, but not quite quickly enough. Tiger threw one off balance with her huge forepaws. She killed the deer with one massive bite to the throat.

Tiger hoisted the deer up with her jaws and dragged it across the meadow to the forest. There in the shade of the trees she began her feast. "A-O-O-O-N-H!" she roared triumphantly. "A-O-O-O-N-H!" Perhaps the big male would join her

later but for now, Tiger's first kill was hers alone. As the hot sun rose high in the lazy sky, Tiger crouched down and gorged. She had a new home. She had food. She was content.

SPOT THE DIFFERENCE

Can you spot ten differences between these two pictures?

TIGER MASK

There are lots of ways to decorate masks. Here are a few things to try.

wool
string
straws
crayons
paint
fabric
coloured paper

Try making a mask. It's easy to do and fun to wear. All you need is a piece of card or thick paper, a length of elastic, string or lace and a pair of scissors.

Draw a basic mask shape on to the card. Remember to make two holes for your eyes and a small hole at each side of the mask. Carefully cut out your mask shape and then decide how you are going to decorate it. Try some of the ideas in the picture on the left. When your mask is decorated, thread the elastic, string or lace through the two holes at the side of the mask. Now your mask is ready to wear!

▶ This mask was made by cutting out the basic shape from card and decorating it with coloured paper.

TIGER STRIPE MAZE

Can you help this baby tiger find its mother?

TRUE OR FALSE?

Which of these facts are true and which ones are false? If you have read this book carefully, you will know the answers.

1. A male tiger may be longer than a car.

2. Female tigers are bigger than male tigers.

3. Every tiger has a different pattern of black stripes on its face.

4. Tigers don't like the cold. They live only in hot places.

5. Tigers live in Africa.

6. A tiger scratches tree trunks to sharpen and clean its claws.

7. A tiger hates to get its feet wet.

8. Tigers like to eat rotting meat.

9. A tiger's favourite food is deer and wild pigs.

10. Tigers usually hunt during the day.

11. A tigress usually has 7 cubs at one time.

12. You can tell how old a tiger is by counting the number of stripes on its tail.

Answers: 1. True; 2. False; 3. True; 4. False; 5. False; 6. True; 7. False; 8. True; 9. True; 10. False; 11. False; 12. False.

INDEX

Asia 6

baby 13
birth 13

camouflage 6
cat 4,12
claws 4,7,8,12
communication 12,14
conservation 17
cubs 13,14,15,16

daytime 10,11
deer 8,9,15
drinking 10

enemies 13
eyes 13

face markings 4
female 4,12,13,14,15,16
food 8,9,13,14,15,16
forests 4,6,16,17
fur 4,6,11

grooming 11
growth 14,15,16

home 7,14
hunting 6,8,9,14,15,16

India 6

jungle 4,6,16

male 4,12
mating 12,13

milk 13
mother 13,14,15,16
mountains 6

nature reserves 17
night 8,15

paw prints 7
pet cat 12
play 16
pouncing 8,9,16
Project Tiger 17

radio collar 17
roaring 7,12

scent marking 7,12
Siberian tigers 6
size 4,13
sleeping 10,14
snow 6
stripes 4,6
swimming 11

tail 4,7
teeth 8,9,12
territory 7
tigress 4,12,13,14,15
tracks 7

weight 4,13
white tigers 4
World Wide Fund
  for Nature 17

zoo tigers 4,17